GW01465814

PLAN

NEW

CONGREGATIONS

a practical guide for Methodists

GRAHAM HORSLEY

METHODIST CHURCH HOME MISSION

First published 1994
Copyright © The Methodist Church Home Mission Division, 1994

ISBN 0 901015 25 3

Printed in Great Britain by
Blackfords of Cornwall, Holmbush Industrial Estate
St Austell, Cornwall PL25 3JL

Contents

1. Introduction   5

2. Where should a new congregation be established?   10

3. Who will join a new congregation?   13

4. Who will lead a new congregation?   16

5. Where should a new congregation meet?   20

6. Develop a plan   24
    Timetable
    Finance
    Resources/Training

7. Develop a structure   27

Appendix One   — House Congregations   30

Appendix Two   — Conference resolutions on church
                  planting   35

Appendix Three — 10 DAWN Principles for responsible
                  church planting   36

Bibliography   38

1 Introduction

Why plant a new congregation?

For most of this century Methodism has been more concerned with church closure than church planting, partly because of the duplication of premises following the unification of the Wesleyan, Primitive and United Methodist Churches in 1932, and partly because of the general decline in church attendance experienced by most denominations.

However, new churches are being planted throughout Britain in increasing numbers. In 1992 the Methodist Conference passed a resolution encouraging every circuit to consider planting a new congregation by the year 2000. At the present time there are at least 30 new Methodist congregations being planted in the United Kingdom. The Church of England is establishing a new congregation every two weeks; the Baptist Church has established a training course for church planters at Spurgeons College.

Why is there this new interest in planting churches? How can a typical Methodist circuit respond? This booklet attempts to help by answering this question in very practical terms. There is a growing body of literature on the theology of church planting which may be consulted.[1] However, most of the literature assumes either an Anglican parish model or a congregational model and this is not always easily applied within the Methodist system. The aim of this booklet is to translate some of the practical advice given in these books into a form which takes into account the Methodist circuit system, to provide the minimum of information to help circuits begin the task of identifying the potential for new congregations, and to indicate where more help may be found.

---

[1] See bibliography on page 38 for some suggestions.

A brief history of church planting

Church planting in the New Testament

The New Testament picture of church planting is not at all easy to discern. We are often given few practical details of how new churches were begun and where we are given information it is usually only partial. Sometimes we are told who was in the church planting team, sometimes how long the initial stay by the apostles lasted. However, to gain a full picture we must piece together a jigsaw puzzle of different snippets of information from the various accounts of churches being planted, particularly in the Acts of the Apostles. The New Testament pattern of church planting appears to be extremely pragmatic. The apostles' primary objective was to make people into disciples of Jesus Christ, and their evangelistic methods were adapted in order to maximise their effectiveness. Their methods varied according to the resources available in the church planting team and the situation in which the church was being planted. It is not possible to provide one biblical church planting blue-print which will apply in all circumstances. However, there are a number of consistent factors which are worth noting.

1. Church planting was sponsored by strong centres. A recurrent theme in the book of Acts is a period of dramatic growth (Jerusalem Acts 2-4, Antioch Acts 13, Ephesus Acts 19). This resulted in a strong local church which would then commission teams to be sent out to new areas. Church planting was not an act of desperation on the part of a shrinking church, it was a result of the vision of the Kingdom of God on the part of a strong church.

2. Church planting was normally done by teams. Paul worked with a variable number of companions in the different situations where he established churches.[2] When solitary evangelists began a work (eg Philip Acts 8), support was normally provided quite quickly from other churches. The team members were able to support one another, and to provide complementary gifts. For instance, Paul had the prophetic edge which led to an uncompromising attitude towards the commitment· of those with whom he worked. Barnabas on the other hand had a pastor's approach

---

[2] cf Acts 13 - Paul, Barnabas, Mark; Acts 16 - Paul, Silas, Timothy, Luke; Acts 18 - Paul, Silas, Timothy, Aquila, Priscilla; Acts 19 - Gaius, Timothy, Tychicus, Trophimus, Erastus, Paul, Luke.

which tended to see and encourage the potential in others even in the face of their failures. This led to a disagreement over the suitability of John Mark (Acts 15:37-41). Despite the possibility of disagreement, it is this variety within teams which gave the new churches breadth of vision and depth of fellowship.

3. Church planting started with those who were already sympathetic. Paul began his ministry in each new place at the synagogue or in the Jewish community with those who would understand at least something of the expectations of the Messiah. Sometimes this was immediately fruitful and led to a Christianisation of the local Jewish/God-fearing community; sometimes it led to the separation of the new Christian community from the existing Jewish one. Using the nucleus found in this way, the church planting team then reached out into the Gentile community.

4. Each new church was allowed to adopt a style which was culturally relevant to the community it sought to evangelise. The Jerusalem council (Acts 15) was primarily concerned with this issue. It was not purely a Jew/Gentile issue, it was an issue of whether or not the church planters were to be allowed autonomy within a given cultural setting. This demonstrates the effectiveness of the church planters in reaching beyond the culturally Jewish groups and evangelising communities from very different cultural settings. This produced a conflict of cultures which could only be resolved by a serious effort to separate the heart of the Good News of Jesus from the traditional cultural and religious practices in which it had been carried.

5. Evangelism in the New Testament is seen primarily as a group activity. Families (Acts 10, 16) and communities (Acts 8:8, 9:35, 14:8) are seen becoming disciples. This contrasts markedly with the very individualistic approach to evangelism which has characterised the twentieth century. Church planting will only be truly effective when families and communities are won for Christ. This point needs considerable thought in developing a 20th century church planting strategy. One of the key elements in this strategy is evangelising the opinion shapers in a community.

6. A newly planted church quickly became autonomous in terms of local leadership, though retaining support from the apostolic network. Paul founded a number of churches but only stayed for a relatively short time before moving on (typically one or two years). The fact that the leadership was both local and autonomous allowed the local congregation to adapt its lifestyle to maximise its impact on the local community. The period of 'cross-cultural' evangelism and paternalistic dependency was kept as short as possible.

Church planting in Methodism

The history of Methodism has been punctuated by periods of intense church planting activity. First of all in the Wesleyan period, with the establishment of 'Societies' (ie new congregations) meeting initially in borrowed buildings. Almost immediately Methodists began to build 'Preaching Houses' as a physical focus for the new congregations.

A second wave of church planting took place in the early 19th century as the Primitive Methodists began first of all with their American style camp meetings at Mow Cop, then with the building of Primitive Methodist chapels.

In the 20th Century the 'Forward Movement' established the large Central Halls with a ministry tailored to meet both the spiritual and the social needs of the day.

In the post-war years the new towns and estates which sprang up to meet the housing needs of the large city overflow population were provided with churches which were much simpler and more utilitarian in style, with a reliance on dual-purpose halls. These church planting movements (and many more) were the attempt of Methodists of that particular period responding to the challenge of Jesus to "Go, then, to all peoples everywhere and make them my disciples. . . " (Matt 28:19 GNB).

And now . . .

The world in which the church witnesses today is very different from that of the New Testament or even the world of the 1950s. Population shifts, urban decay and regeneration have dramatically altered the communities in which many people live. In some areas (both urban and rural) the church has withdrawn altogether. Buildings have been sold and a generation has grown up totally outside the influence of the church. This is most clearly highlighted in the alarming decline of the churches' work with young people (cf *All God's Children*, National Society/Church House Publishing for a thorough survey). In some areas there are congregations which are meeting these challenges. In others, large sections of the population are effectively unchurched because no one is reaching out to them in Jesus' name. Planting new congregations is one of the ways in which this task may be done. If church planting is to become an effective evangelistic method for Methodists in the closing years of the 20th century, there are a number of different areas where new skills must be acquired. This booklet tries to outline those areas and point to places where more experience can be found.

It is important to emphasise that we are talking about planting new congregations, not just about building new churches. There are many different ways of beginning a new congregation; it may mean building a new Methodist or ecumenical church in a particular location; it may mean establishing a new congregation inside an existing building; it may mean beginning a work on secular premises or in members' homes. Perhaps the greatest challenge facing the Christian Church in the closing years of the 20th century is to dream dreams and see visions. If this booklet enables circuits to begin to bring their visions to reality, it will have achieved its purpose.

It is also important to note that any attempt to establish a new congregation carries a risk of failure. It may be that success will come only after a time of failure. This is particularly true in an area where the circuit, the local churches and the Christians involved may have to learn new skills. Perhaps an important contribution of the church planting movement is to encourage Christians to risk failure for the sake of the Kingdom of God. If a new venture does fail it is important that we examine the reasons for failure so that a subsequent venture has a greater chance of success.

2 Where should a new congregation be established?

Is there the potential for a new congregation in every circuit in Methodism? The 1992 Methodist Conference challenged every circuit to consider planting a new congregation by the year 2000. If this challenge is to be met then there are a number of possibilities which a circuit could examine.

Look at your neighbourhood

Surveys show that approximately 10% of the population of Britain are regular churchgoers so it would seem logical that an unchurched population of 2000 is capable of supporting a new congregation, and one of 500 may do so in appropriate circumstances.

A circuit policy group could usefully spend time analysing a large scale map of the circuit on which are marked the churches of the area (not just Methodist) and their catchment areas. Often the catchment area is not simply the housing closest to the church—different churches tend to attract certain types of people from the surrounding area; for instance a church in a mixed housing area might be reaching the occupants of one type of housing but not another which is equally close to the building!

Next, mark any areas of housing which have been built in the last 5-10 years, and any proposed new developments (the local council will have a development plan which should be generally available). The map should also mark any boundaries which people find it hard to cross (dual carriageways, bypasses, railways or rivers all effectively cut areas in half so a congregation may be needed on both sides of the boundary). Try to find out where people naturally refer to (which shops, schools, pubs, post offices are used by people on a housing development?). Is there already a church serving this reference point within the community (again, not just Methodist)?

If within the circuit boundaries there is an area of 500+ houses which are effectively unchurched, then a new congregation should be seriously considered. This may be a new estate or a town-centre redevelopment. Perhaps there is a large council estate which has a church on its edge, but the church only attracts worshippers from private housing nearby (often despite a large number of baptismal/wedding/funeral contacts on the council estate). If so, then a new congregation may be needed which is specifically reaching into the council estate. In rural circuits there may well be villages where the Methodist chapel has ceased to hold services but where a more contemporary style of worship might plant a new congregation in an old building.

From this survey it may be possible to identify potential catchment areas for a new congregation.

Often the approach is not the formal one identified above but an informal one coming from an individual or a church which identifies an area in its neighbourhood as having the potential for a new congregation. This will need confirming by the more formal methods outlined above, but has the advantage of an individual or a group committed to the project from the outset.

Look at the existing churches

A second important area to consider is the existing churches in the circuit. Church growth research has consistently shown that a church which is more than 80% full at its principal service has reached a level of attendance which discourages new people from joining.

There is also a considerable amount of evidence which shows that 180-200 members is a point at which a church must adopt a very different style of leadership or cease to grow. The church must then face the question of the best method of growing beyond this size. Should it change its leadership style to a more structured, formal style of corporate leadership acknowledging that no individual can have an intimate pastoral knowledge of the whole congregation, and that the congregation cannot know one another in a way which will encourage close fellowship? Perhaps it might be preferable to look at ways of regrouping the church into a different congregational structure.

If there are churches in the circuit which have reached either of these critical points, then it may be time to consider establishing a new congregation. This might take the form of planting a new congregation in a slightly different area (a survey of where the membership comes from ought to highlight possibilities).

However, it may be preferable to plant a new congregation in the existing building. Within the Methodist Church today there is a wide variety of styles of worship, and often tensions within a local church as to how that variety is to be celebrated. Several churches have found that the best way forward is to allow different services to take on different characteristics to meet the needs of different groups within the community. The impetus for this may come from an analysis of the needs of the congregation, or it may come from the pressure of a building which is full.[3]

This stage of surveying the possibilities needs to be done carefully, and in a way that involves as many people as possible from the outset. If there is a circuit policy group already meeting, then this would naturally fall within their remit; if not, it may be advisable to set up a working group from the circuit meeting so that its deliberations will include all who are interested.

At this survey stage it is important to engage in ecumenical consultation. If another church is beginning to plan a similar venture it is good to begin the project as a joint initiative. It is important to set ecumenical wheels turning early as almost all churches which have been planted as LEPs[4] express frustration at the amount of time taken by sponsoring groups to finalise agreements! In the early stages the local churches involved will need to work out the best way of going forward together—should the plant begin as a formal LEP or should it begin as an informal venture and then become an LEP later on? The District Chairman and the District Ecumenical Secretary will be able to advise on this.[5]

---

[3] cf *In the Crucible* and *On the Anvil*, both by Robert Warren and published by Highland Books, for one example of a church which has grown in this way.

[4] What is an LEP?

A Local Ecumenical Project (LEP) comes into being when co-operation between different churches in a particular locality or institution is officially recognised by the denominational authorities of the churches involved. It may take the form of shared buildings, shared congregational life, shared ministry, a local covenant or any combination of these.

[5] *Planting Tomorrow's Churches Today*, Appendices A and B offer very practical advice on assessing the relative need for church planting, and for conducting a community survey to see if the community is receptive to a church plant, and to help determine what style of plant is appropriate.

3 Who will join a new congregation?

To identify a catchment area is not the same as identifying a catchment people. All churches have a bias to a particular group within their locality. They may not always recognise this (and may vehemently deny it) but even unconsciously churches develop programmes which reinforce the preferences of their congregation and therefore are most effective at attracting people with similar tastes. If this is true in a given situation, then it is also true that other groups within the community feel marginalised. They may be present within the church (often at odds with the rest of the congregation), they may have already 'voted with their feet', or they may never have been a part of the worshipping community. If this group can be identified within the community, it may require a new congregation with an appropriate ethos to be developed in order to draw them into the life of the church.

Identifying a target group

A number of circuits have found that a village chapel with a small, elderly congregation and a very traditional worship style has made little impact upon the local community, but it has been possible to plant alongside it a new congregation based on all-age worship using a younger planting team from other parts of the circuit—they have effectively targeted a different group within the community. This is not to deny the validity of the worship of the existing group; it is simply accepting that different groups within the community require a different approach.

The dilemma of how to target a group within the community is often at its most painful when a group of people travel a considerable distance to keep an inner-city church going but, by their different expectations and cultural values, actually prevent an indigenous congregation from developing. One URC congregation in Liverpool has tackled this problem by having a condition of membership that each member lives within walking distance of the church![6] An advantage of planning to evangelise a target

---

6 cf *Ten New Churches* Chapt 4 Anfield Road Fellowship, Ed. Roger Forster.

group within the community in this way is that it may be possible to use existing premises to evangelise a very different group within the same community by offering a range of worship styles within one church building.[7]

This approach may pose problems for our theological understanding of the church. If we believe that Christ has made us one, how can we worship in separate groups? The answer to this question is too complicated to be fully covered here, but most churches already cater for a minority of their local community and, whatever the style of worship, there will always be those who feel excluded. In the end the dilemma may not be 'can we all worship together?', but 'will some of us worship at all?'! To recognise this in a positive way and to work to provide a meaningful way of communicating the Good News to those who feel excluded at present is part of the answer. If there is more than one congregation using one building, the leadership must work very hard to celebrate the things which the congregations have in common as well as encouraging them to develop their own spirituality. It won't always be easy but it must be attempted, and the attitude and example of the leadership is all-important.

If the target group is clearly identified from the outset, it is easier to select the right evangelistic methods and the right worship, nurture and pastoral styles to reach this group effectively. Most of the circuits which have planted new churches comment that their styles of worship have evolved from the traditional 'five hymn sandwich' in order to reach people with no history of church going. However, there does not appear to be one consistent pattern emerging. A recent survey of some thirty new congregations in the Methodist Church revealed that some churches major on all-age worship, others on high levels of participation, others on evangelistic preaching, yet others on 'charismatic' worship in which the supernatural gifts of the Holy Spirit are encouraged. This variety reflects the different groups who are being targeted and the particular gifts of the planting group.

Reaching the unchurched

It is important to ensure that the church is ministering to the needs felt by the community it serves. This is obvious in terms of the church's pastoral ministry, but has not always been clearly recognised within the church's

---

[7] cf *In the Crucible*, Robert Warren, for a description of how this works in an Anglican/Baptist LEP in Sheffield.

teaching ministry. This becomes especially relevant if the church is making a determined effort to reach those who have little connection with traditional Christianity.[8] Fortunately there are many issues which are of common concern to those people both within and without traditional church structures.

A good example of this was the concern expressed at the 1993 Methodist Conference about the pressures upon families and especially parents. It is important to deal with the issues of family life as an integral part of the church's teaching programme. Recent initiatives by the Division of Education and Youth in the area of parenting are well worth exploring.[9] It is inevitable that teaching on marriage, the family and children will be painful for many people but if they are already wounded it may be a necessary part of their healing. Teaching which is both relevant and biblically based is an important part of helping people to grow in faith and helps to build bridges as people struggle to find faith.

A very practical demonstration of this may be the difficulty experienced by the children of broken marriages in worshipping on Sundays. If Sunday is also access day for estranged fathers it may be that a new congregation has to think about the day for worship as well as the time and place.

When considering how the church relates to families it is important to recognise that the way in which the church treats people who approach it for marriage or baptism sends very clear signals into the community. Too often this issue is left to the discretion of the minister and is not an issue on which the church has worked out a policy. It is worth checking how many people who have joined the local church in the last five years were won to faith by baptismal or marriage contacts—this ought to be a fruitful area of evangelism. It is even better to talk to families who have recently joined the church after the welcome they experienced and see what lessons need to be learnt. If there are no new members then the matter may be even more urgent.

---

[8] cf *A World Apart: Creating a Church for the Unchurched,* Martin Robinson, published Monarch/CPAS for a good discussion of these issues.

[9] *Partners in Parenting*: for details contact Methodist Division of Education and Youth, 2 Chester House, Pages Lane, Muswell Hill, London N10 1PR. Tel 081-444 9845.

4 Who will lead a new congregation?

Of all the factors involved in planting a new church, this is almost certainly the most crucial. It is also one in which there are a large number of possible ways forward. The local leadership must take time to explore the options in this area:

A solo church planter (or married couple)

During the new town and overspill estate boom of the 50s and 60s, this was probably the most common method. A minister (and family) or in more recent years a deacon(ess) or lay worker were provided with a house in the middle of a new estate and given the task of finding local Christians, evangelising non-Christians and starting a church. This method gives the church planter almost total freedom to react to the needs of the community. The disadvantage is that it can be a terribly isolated existence and places considerable stress on the church planter. It is also a very slow method of establishing a congregation since the whole of a new congregation must be built up from scratch.

A small team

This may either be a small team coming from right outside the local situation, or a team recruited from within the local area. An incoming team will probably only number three to six people, whereas a small local team may be six to ten members. The itinerant small team is one of the methods most frequently used in Acts of the Apostles. It has been revived in recent years by most of the denominations and a number of para-church organisations. The Seed Team programme within Methodism will provide small teams of people (normally three or four) to work with a local church in pioneer evangelistic work.[10] This has the advantage of being small enough to react flexibly in a given situation, and yet big enough to provide an embryo Christian community to build upon. It is vital that this team

---

[10] For details of the Seed Team Programme contact Rob Frost, Raynes Park Methodist Church, Tolverne Road, London SW20 8RA; tel. 081-944 7729.

is located in the area where the church is being planted so that it can quickly build a network of contacts and friendships in the local community as a precursor to its evangelistic work. The disadvantage of bringing a team in from the outside is that its members may take some time to adjust to the local culture, and that they have only a limited time to offer (normally one or two years for a Seed Team).

A locally based team has most of the advantages outlined above, but may not have all the members resident in the catchment area. This makes it much harder to build up the circle of friendships which successful evangelism demands. However, a local team will normally understand the local culture better and will not have such tight time constraints upon them. They may well become the leadership of the new church and stay there semi-permanently. On the other hand, they may set themselves the target of creating a new local leadership within a five year period so as to be released themselves for further church planting.

A larger locally based team

It may well be possible to locate a number of local Christians (typically 15-50) who would be willing to commit themselves to a new church plant. If this is to happen, then three factors must be clearly defined as soon as possible:

1. How will the team be selected? On the grounds that they volunteer, or that they have the right gifts and experience? Immature or disaffected members of the local church are unlikely to be good church planters. A team must have a balance of people with evangelistic, pastoral, worship-leading and leadership skills. It's also a biblical principle that we give of our best, not our leftovers.

2. How will the sending church cope? If the church is in an area of rapid growth, it may be that new people will come quickly to fill the vacated positions. In one current Methodist church plant, a main impetus behind the plant was that the church leadership recognised leadership gifts in members which were not being used because of a surfeit of skilled people— not every church will be so fortunate. Many churches which have sent out teams to plant new churches have experienced a time of bereavement in the mother church.

3. How will they relate to the local community in which they are working? If a large proportion of the team are not locally resident, there is a real danger that the new congregation exists independently of the local community and dies out within a generation.

Team leadership

If there is a single issue which determines whether a new congregation will thrive or fail, it is the quality of its leadership. In a recent study of six failed church plants by the Baptist Church, the prime cause of failure was identified as inadequate leadership.[11] Stuart Christine identifies the qualities of a church plant leader as:

* ★ Called and envisioned by God. Church planting is God's work.

* ★ An ability to inspire others to catch the vision.

* ★ An ability to draw up action plans to achieve vision goals.

* ★ Resourcefulness and organisational ability to make things work.

* ★ Hardworking and resilient. Foundations are hard work, often with little to show on the surface.

* ★ Prayerful—foundations must follow the architect's design.[12]

The leader will be recognised as a mature Christian within the local church and will have a track record of completing projects effectively. As the leadership role is so important and will be a very large commitment it will almost certainly necessitate the leader being released from other duties.

The leader may be ordained or lay, the personality is more important. The circuit will need to define clearly his/her duties within the circuit structures so as to create the necessary freedom for the new role.

Although the leader may be the most important appointment to a church planting team, there are other gifts which are essential within the team:

* ★ *Evangelism*—all Christians are witnesses, but only some have the God-given talent for leading others to faith. The Bible Society's Church Growth research suggests that 10% of Christians have this gift. At least one team member should be an evangelist.

* ★ *Pastor*—a new congregation will need a lot of encouragement. A pastoral heart within the team is essential to nurture those who are brought in by the evangelist.

* ★ *Hospitality*—team members with this gift will be good at building bridges into the community which is being evangelised.

---

11 cf *Planting Tomorrow's Churches Today,* Stuart Christine and Martin Robinson, Monarch, p 209.
12 *Planting Tomorrow's Churches Today,* Stuart Christine and Martin Robinson, Monarch, pp 212-3.

* *Worship leader*—once a congregation begins to announce a Sunday Service (which may not be for some time), the gift of leading worship becomes one of the 'shop-window' gifts for the new church. It may be that a local preacher or minister can be set aside for this role; it may be that someone with ability needs to be identified and trained early on in the planning stage.

* *Workers with Children and Young People*—this job may be especially challenging if the premises used for the new congregation are small. The whole team will need to plan carefully the interaction between the young people's work and the other activities of the congregation.

It is also important that the team has a clearly defined structure. In the early days of a church plant flexibility is important, but if there are not clear channels of decision making and communication flexibility can be lost in confusion!

The above description may seem so demanding that St Peter and St Paul would think twice about volunteering—at the end of the day a sense of call is probably the most important qualification for a team member, coupled with a flexibility which will allow the team members to change and develop as the new congregation grows. A person with a very dogmatic, fixed personality may be invaluable in some situations, but is unlikely to work well in a church planting team. Above all team members need a sense of proportion and the faith that God's grace is made perfect in our weakness.

5 Where should a new congregation meet?

If a church plant is to be carried out in a new development, one of the key questions is whether to plan to build a 'church' or to hire/adapt premises, or to do a combination of the two. However, be warned that in the present economic climate developers and councils do not often put aside land for community usage. If you want to earmark a prime site, you will have to start early in the development and persist long and hard if you are to be successful.

Conrad Hilton is reputed to have commented that there are only three things that are important for the success of a hotel—*location, location and location!* Similarly for churches?

However, not all church plants are on new developments so there are a number of options to be considered:

Existing church premises

The fact that an existing congregation has ceased to meet does not mean there is no potential for a new church. There are a number of new churches which have been planted in existing buildings. It may be that the existing premises need extensive refurbishment before a new congregation is begun. However, it may be that a new style of worship, a new time for the principal service or a new leadership group are all that is required.

In assessing the suitability of existing premises there are two main factors to be considered: first, their suitability for the style of worship envisaged by the new congregation and, secondly, the impact they will have on new worshippers. It may be worth inviting a complete stranger to walk round the premises identifying any attractive features and more importantly any off-putting ones!

It may well be that the premises are to be shared initially (eg there is an elderly group who meet on Sunday afternoons only and the circuit propose to start a Sunday morning all-age service to draw in new families who've moved into the area) in which case a good deal of sensitivity will be needed in moving forward.

Private homes

If there are already Christians living in the target area, then one of the best ways to start may well be home-based evangelism. Is this an end in itself (cf House Congregation information in Appendix One) or a step along the way to a bigger group? It is quite possible that there are a number of situations where effective evangelism demands a Christian presence in a very specific location but the catchment community is incapable of supporting a fully developed church. In this situation a home-based fellowship group feeding into and supported by the nearest local church may be the best long-term solution.

Hire premises

Schools, community halls, sports centres and pub concert rooms have all been used as home to new churches. There a number of advantages and disadvantages.

Advantages

1. *Cheapness*—£20-30 per session may seem a lot, but not when compared to the £100,000+ cost of a new building. This enables a circuit to take a step of faith (or a risk!) safe in the knowledge that failure will not mean financial disaster.

2. *Accessibility*—for many non-churchgoers a church is a frightening place. It has rules and rituals that they don't understand. A school hall on the other hand is familiar territory. This of course has disadvantages as well as advantages—it would be difficult to evangelise a school-phobic from a school hall based church!

3. *Low maintenance*—many churches spend most of their planning time on building problems; if these are looked after by someone else there is more time/energy for mission.

4. *Efficiency*—is it good stewardship to own and maintain a building which is used for only one or two days a week?

5. *Contacts*—by using a community facility you will almost certainly forge stronger links with the community.

Disadvantages

1. *Inconvenience*—the premises may not be available at the best times (eg mid-week youth work, morning mums and tots).

2. *Unsuitability*—churches often feel 'prayed-in', halls often feel cold and bare. In the first few weeks of a church plant, arriving early with a boot full of hymn-books, Bible, PA gear and lecterns, and spending an hour setting up the room may be fine. After two or three years of doing this, enthusiasm may begin to fail!

3. *Image*—for some people at least, a church which meets in a hired hall has a sense of impermanence about it—it's not quite a proper church! This will need countering by the lifestyle of the members and imagination in adapting the premises (eg the use of banners can transform a bare hall).

4. *Inflexibility*—a purpose-built church should actually say something about the congregation's understanding of worship. It can be designed to use visual images in key places (eg a cross, a communion table, a pulpit, banners etc.) and will be arranged to seat people to maximise fellowship, or to focus their attention on the cross or the preacher. In a hired hall other constraints may make it difficult to present the right setting for worship—this will need careful thought.

Temporary buildings

These are now a familar sight outside schools, libraries and offices. They are relatively cheap to erect (under £40,000 for multi-purpose facilities for 80 people) yet can be extremely comfortable. They have the advantage of round-the-clock availability and low maintenance costs. They are an excellent middle step to house a new congregation which has begun to grow using homes or hired facilities but is not yet ready to undertake a full-scale development project. The disadvantage is that it represents a considerable investment if the plant fails and yet is not a long-term solution if the work thrives!

A purpose-built new building

This is probably most peoples' first thought when a church plant is discussed, but it represents such a huge commitment in terms of finance, time and planning that it is probably best considered when a new church has proved its viability in one of the ways outlined above—with the proviso that negotiations for a site will normally need to be pursued early in a new development. However, a site is not such a risk as a completed building as it may be resold.

If a circuit is considering the renting, leasing, purchase or building of premises, consultation with the Property Division should take place at the earliest stage. The Division has wide experience, knowledge of funds available and a number of helpful publications.[13]

Conclusion

If a circuit is to take a genuine step of faith in church planting, it's best to start out on one of the low-cost low-planning premises as this frees time for mission and leaves more expensive schemes until later.

---

[13] Methodist Church Property Division, Central Buildings, Oldham Street, Manchester M1 1JQ. Tel: 061-236 5194. Fax: 061-236 0752.

6 Develop a plan

Although eventual responsibility for a new congregation may be devolved upon the Christians who live in a particular area or are members of a particular church, a new congregation is most likely to succeed if it is seen to be part of circuit policy. In some areas there may be potential for more than one new congregation in which case the circuit will need to think carefully about which should be given priority. The talent available across a circuit will almost always produce a better team than would be possible within one church.

Timetable

The following elements should be considered as a circuit begins to plan a church plant. Care taken in the advance planning will almost certainly save heartache later on. You only get one chance to make a first impression!

1. Assess the need

The best way to assess the need is to talk to people in the area of the proposed plant.[14] It's important not to rely on supposition about an area. Spend time getting to know it well.

2. Establish a method

This will mean working out the style of the plant, checking availability of suitable premises, identifying and recruiting a team, working out an evangelistic strategy and setting an appropriate timetable. The evangelistic strategy of the new congregation requires careful thought. The excellent literature on *Finding Faith Today*[15] may help the leaders to understand the factors which help people to become Christians, and the process by which conversion usually happens.[16]

---

[14] A useful guide to a community survey can be found in *Planting Tomorrow's Churches Today* p 343-347.

The Bible Society has a computer data base with a considerable amount of information about the whole country; for details, contact them at Stonehill Green, Westlea, Swindon SN5 5DG. Tel: 0793 513713.

[15] *Finding Faith Today*, ed. John Finney, published Bible Society.

[16] See Bibliography for further suggestions of helpful evangelistic material.

3. Establish a presence

There are two types of publicity: personal and impersonal—both are important. Impersonal publicity will involve delivering leaflets and putting up posters about the new church plant. It will also involve publicity in local papers (don't forget 'free' newspapers) and on local radio community programmes. Personal publicity will involve door-to-door visitation, setting up house-groups or coffee mornings/evenings. It will need research to discover what contacts already exist in the new area with people who are friendly towards the church (a search through baptismal, wedding and funeral records of neighbouring churches may well be a good starting place).

4. Train the leaders

Worship leaders, pastoral visitors, nurture group leaders and others with leadership responsibilities all need training. Some people on the team may already be doing these jobs in local churches, others may not. Either way it is likely that training will be involved as replacements will be needed for any people being released.

5. Set an official opening date

Make this count—you only start once. Some thought will need to be given as to the best time for this.[17] Do bear in mind that a team may need to begin praying, training, preparing and even evangelising well in advance of the beginning of a public worship service.

6. Pray throughout!

This is an aspect of the church plant in which the whole circuit can share. Involve as many people as possible in as imaginative a way as possible. It is important to keep prayers informed—try to establish regular prayer bulletins around the circuit.

Finance

Most new congregations in Methodism start small and rely on local funding only. Budgets for a small low-key church plant are typically £2000 or less. Most large developments are planted ecumenically and apply for local and national funding for buildings and personnel. Circuits which are planning to extend their work should approach the Home Mission Division for advice and information on grants. The Property Division welcomes enquiries about buildings and funding their construction or improvement. The Connexional

---

[17] cf *Planting Tomorrow's Churches Today*—chapt. 12, page 281.

Advance and Priority Fund makes grants for personnel and property (see Standing Orders 970-977 for its criteria).[18]

Resources/Training

At the moment Methodism has few formal resources for church planting training. The Baptist Church has a training course at Spurgeon's College & YWAM run residential training courses at St Helens which may accept Methodists. There is a growing body of resource literature (see appended Bibliography). However, much of the training will need to be done locally by trying new things, reflecting, assessing and modifying as the plant goes along. In this way, the church plant will become more truly indigenous.

The Home Mission Division has recently established a church planting steering group which is hoping to act as a focus for the development of church planting within Methodism. There is also a connexional register of new congregations—there may be one close by who will share their experiences with you. For details contact Rev Brian Hoare, Home Mission Division, 1 Central Buildings, Westminster SW1H 9NH. Tel. 071-222 8010.

The Seed Team programme is able to provide small teams to help in all kinds of pioneer evangelism including establishing new congregations. For details contact Rev Rob Frost, Raynes Park Methodist Church, Tolverne Road, London SW20 8RA. Tel. 081-944 5678 or 081-944 7729.

DAWN (Discipling A Whole Nation) is an inter-church group committed to church planting as a means of evangelism. They publish a regular newsletter and hold congresses from time to time. They can be contacted at: Challenge 2000, 107 Stanstead Road, Forest Hill, London SE23 1HH. Tel. 081-291 6087.

Bible Society offers a variety of training courses in all areas of Church Growth, including church planting, and is willing to lead a seminar appropriate to local needs.

---

[18] Applications for grants need to be channelled via Circuit Meeting, District Policy Committee and District Synod. Contact District Home Mission Secretary and District Policy Committee Secretary for advice. See also SO 312 and SO 975. It is also advisable to consult with the Chairman of the District as soon as plans are begun.

7 Develop a structure

A new church plant needs to be integrated into and supported by the circuit. It also needs to be sufficiently independent to try new methods. Several problems must be addressed if this is to work in practice.

1. Evangelistic strategy

Some new churches set out to recreate a typical Methodist church in an area of new housing. They recruit principally by appealing to Christians who have recently moved into the area and not yet transferred membership to a local church, or by reaching people with a Christian background but who have drifted away from commitment to a local church (ie. transfer or reinstatement growth). Other new churches set out to share the good news of Jesus with people from right outside the traditional church culture (ie conversion growth). A church with the former evangelistic strategy could quite quickly be expected to become a 'normal' church on the circuit plan, whereas one with the latter may need very different treatment if is is to flourish.

2. Is it a House Congregation, a class meeting or a society?

Most Methodists are familiar with the structure of a society or local Methodist church which is under the pastoral oversight of a circuit minister, has preachers appointed according to the circuit plan, runs activities determined by the local church council and makes a contribution to the circuit budget; and a class meeting which is a group within a local church which meets under the leadership of a class leader appointed by the church council for fellowship, teaching and pastoral support. The House Congregation, however, may be less familiar yet offers many advantages (cf Appendix 1 p25ff).

1. There is a defined system of accountability with freedom.
2. There is room to do different things in worship.
3. There is reassessment as the new congregation grows.

A new congregation could be any one of the three, it may even be all three as it grows from a class to a House Congregation, then finally a society. It may need the freedom to exist as a House Congregation for some considerable time.

3. How will the new congregation relate to the plan?

A survey of recent church plants has shown that worship leaders who are easily identified and who provide a consistent link with new worshippers are vital in the early days of a plant. This will probably mean that initially the worship will be arranged differently from most of the plan (though it may still be featured on the printed plan). Most new churches have set aside a small group of preachers to lead the worship and to provide continuity of teaching and style. The key leadership will therefore probably be lay, and will need to be released from other circuit commitments. The time it takes to place the new church on the plan in a more 'normal' way will depend on a number of factors—principally, the speed at which the congregation grows to become a self-supporting church, and the way in which its worship differs from the other churches in the circuit. The larger the differences, the more carefully it will need to be integrated.

4. How will the new church relate to the circuit budget?

This is not simply a question of whether the new congregation should pay an assessment, and if so how much. If a new church is begun there will inevitably be overheads involved in finding premises—these could be very small (£25 a week to hire a hall) or astronomical (£350,000 to build a new church). If churches in the circuit release key personnel to plant the church, then their financial contribution to the local society could be lost, and often the most gifted workers are the most sacrificial givers! If a lay worker is employed, the salary must be met; if not, one of the circuit ministers will probably invest a lot of time in the new church to the detriment of other causes. This may mean an adjustment of pastoral charge in the circuit.

If a new congregation is to be given space to grow properly, it may need to be freed from any commitment to the circuit budget for a considerable time. If a five year programme of contributions is worked out, beginning at zero and gradually rising by 20% a year to the level of other churches in the circuit, the circuit treasurer may be pleasantly surprised by a new congregation's willingness to pay more. If an assessment is levied too soon, it may place too much strain on a tender shoot and prevent it from growing into a mature plant

. . . and finally!

By now your circuit may be well on the way to planting a new congregation. What if it fails? Would that be a disaster? In earlier days in Methodism it was not at all unusual to see different names both appearing and disappearing on the circuit plan as circuits attempted to evangelise new areas. Pioneer evangelism is a risk venture. If a new congregation is not established as part of the ongoing life of a circuit, there will inevitably be a period of questioning. Did it fail through lack of planning? Or through inadequate leadership? Was it an inappropriate style of worship? Is that area already overchurched? Is it not the right time?

But in the questioning it's also important to discover what positive lessons have been learned. Have new gifts been discovered and released in the circuit team? Have new ideas in worship and evangelism been developed which can be applied elsewhere?

There will also need to be a time of healing for those involved. If they hold themselves responsible for the failure of the new congregation, they will need careful pastoring. A sense of failure can be a powerful motivation to succeed next time if it is channelled correctly. It was the failure of his trip to America that fuelled John Wesley's search for a deeper relationship with God and led to his heart being 'strangely warmed'. For Christians today it may well be that an apparent failure will lead them to a deeper commitment to Christ which will help them overcome personal weaknesses and be better equipped for future ministry.

However, a good deal of effort will be needed to resist the "we tried it once—it didn't work!" syndrome from blighting future attemps.

Appendix One— House Congregations

The report appended below was adopted by the Methodist Conference of 1987 as a basis for churches to experiment with new forms of church life.

House Congregations—a Methodist strategy

From the earliest days of the church, new Christian communities have met in homes. Even when they outgrew the modest accommodation of a private house and began to meet for worship in more spacious premises, the home did not cease to be an important place for Christian meeting. The need was felt both for celebration in large congregations and for the intimate fellowship of smaller groups. As the church reached out into new areas the home was most frequently the initial setting for worship, teaching and prayer.

This pattern is clearly seen in the history of the Methodist movement. The importance of the small group meeting in a home was such that even as Methodism became a separate denomination and began to build churches, the class meeting continued to be a vital part of the lives of Methodist people.

During the last 30 years in Britain, one of the most striking features of church life has been the growth of new Christian congregations based on the home. So significant has this development been that it has become generally referred to as the House Church movement. The danger of such a phrase is its implication that there is one clearly defined phenomenon known as a House Church, whereas in fact the range and variety of such communities is considerable. Most of them are characterised however by the rejection of traditional church life, especially its physical and organisational structures, and an emphasis on personal relationships within the Christian community.

The extent to which the House Church movement is a genuine missionary movement is a matter of debate. Though the number of people belonging to House Churches has risen dramatically, a great many had previously belonged to another denomination. However it is beyond question that a large number of people have become and continued to be Christians through the influence of a House Church congregation, while many more have found their faith renewed and their lives enriched in a way that had not seemed possible within their previous denomination.

Not all that has happened within the House Church movement has been good news. Some congregations have developed authoritarian hierarchical structures which have led to their leadership becoming totalitarian, if not tyrannical. Some have shown little love towards other Christian congregations. Many have become inward looking and smug. At the same time the movement has brought real blessing to many people and has reminded the church as a whole of aspects of the faith which had slipped from view.

The following aspects of the House Church movement have been generally welcomed.

a) The emphasis on caring personal relationships among members of the congregation.
b) The development of new styles of community life and the recognition and releasing of the gifts of all members of the congregation.
c) Spontaneity and informality in worship.
d) A setting in which it is easy to welcome first-time worshippers.
e) Freedom from the burdens of property maintenance.
f) Renewed attention to the doctrine of the Holy Spirit.

In recent years the Home Mission Division has given special attention to 'the missionary shape of the congregation'. It is recognised that there is no blueprint for a model church, rather there is an appropriate shape for a local church according to its circumstances, its history and its opportunities. Moreover different missionary activities require different shapes, and units of different size. The fight against hunger involves national and international networks of churches. Many training programmes draw people from groups of churches, and ministry to a city involves all the churches in that city in concerted planning and action. All the members of a local church meet in one place for worship, study groups may bring a dozen people together, while counselling usually involves just two or three.

In the light of this we have asked ourselves if the Methodist Church is sufficiently flexible to allow for all these possibilities and more. In general we want to affirm that it is, indeed that our constitution is a great deal more flexible than is usually admitted, let alone practised. However it is often said that our Standing Orders reflect the needs of a medium to large local church and tend to impose a heavy administrative burden on smaller congregations. At the same time there is statistical evidence that small churches with under 25 members are less likely to have growing congregations than larger churches.

All these considerations have led us to ask if this is the time to encourage an alternative form of local congregational life. We use the term House Congregations to indicate that our model is not the contemporary House Church movement but the small groups in which Christians have met during the period of the apostolic church, the Methodist revival, and at other times. We invite circuits to consider if, as part of their missionary strategy, it would be appropriate to establish House Congregations as a means of bringing into Christian faith and fellowship those who may not be attracted by existing patterns of church life.

When we reflected on how this might be done we looked at the possibility of proposing a new Standing Order to Conference, but concluded that this would be a controversial and divisive process and that it was in any case unnecessary. The Methodist constitution already allows, as we shall show, for the establishment of House Congregations with sufficient freedom of action to indicate whether or not such a form of local congregational life should have permanent place within the life of the church.

We recommend the following procedure. A circuit meeting may decide, as part of its missionary strategy, to encourage the establishment of a House Congregation or to recognise an existing group of people as a House Congregation within the circuit. In taking such a decision it needs to bear in mind both the needs of the community or communities served by the circuit, and the likely effects of such an innovation on existing churches within the circuit.

Following such a decision by the circuit meeting, those who wish to do so are invited to belong to a local congregation whose normal place of worship is a home or similar convenient meeting place of a small group. The congregation is under the care of a class leader who is a member of the pastoral committee of a local church in the circuit. The congregation will not own property though it may in some instances wish to rent a room or rooms. The circuit meeting will ensure that the House Congregation is represented on it through the provisions of Standing Order 510 (1) (ix). The provisions of Part 8 of Methodist Standing Orders (Membership) will apply. The Sacrament of Holy Communion shall be celebrated by ministers or by those with a formal dispensation under our normal procedures. Those who lead worship in a House Congregation need not be accredited local preachers but must respect Methodist doctrinal standards, and the class leader will be responsible for seeing that this is so. The circuit meeting will make appropriate financial arrangements, and will plan suitable occasions for worship and celebration where members of the House Congregation can express their solidarity with the larger Methodist community. A circuit minister will have overall pastoral responsibility for the House Congregation but will allow it the greatest possible freedom to develop its own patterns of relationship, worship and missionary life.

An essential feature of a House Congregation is its limited size. The circuit meeting will determine the maximum size for a recognised House Congregation in the light of local circumstances. Should a House Congregation grow larger than the permitted maximum it will either become a circuit church or will arrange for its members to re-group into two or more House Congregations. This decision should be taken after the fullest consultation between the House Congregation and the circuit meeting, and in the light of the circuit's missionary strategy.

Other aspects of the relationship between the circuit and the House Congregation are to be decided locally. The responsibilities of the circuit meeting are to satisfy itself:

a) that the class leader is a person who, by conviction and qualification, is able to uphold Methodist doctrinal standards,

b) that the life and witness of the House Congregation is in harmony with the circuit's missionary strategy,

c) that financial arrangements are consistent with Methodism's charitable status.

A number of reservations have been expressed about the proposals for Methodist House Congregations and these will need to be taken into account by the circuits wishing to adopt such a policy. Some are afraid that the experiment might 'get out of hand'. If this means that our present understanding of the nature of the church may be seriously challenged, this is something we should surely welcome. If it means that the Circuit Meeting will lose control, the answer is that what is proposed in the notes makes clear the continuing responsibility of that body.

There is a concern that House Congregations may become inward looking, or gatherings of disgruntled or disaffected Methodists. They risk drawing people from one social class, or with a single theological outlook, thus denying the variety of humanity and the power of God to overcome human divisions and reconcile all people. The impression may be given that it is in House Congregations that the really exciting things are happening, to the detriment of the life of the traditional churches in the circuit. The circuit meeting will need to be aware of these and other dangers and to guard against them. It should take time in the circuit meeting at least once a year to review the life of its House Congregations and to receive the insights and blessings which members of the House Congregations may wish to share with the circuit as a whole.

It is not the job of the Home Mission Division to say where House Congregations should be established; that is the task of the circuit meeting. However there are a number of communities within British society which have proved particularly resistant to the ministry of traditional churches. Some of these communities are defined geographically, eg council housing estates or inner city neighbourhoods, and others are defined culturally, ethnically, or in terms of people's work or life-style. Wherever there are communities whose members are noticeably under-represented in our churches, then there is a prime facie case for considering new forms of local congregational life.

The Home Mission Division is eager to hear from circuits that have House Congregations or are considering their establishment. In this way we hope to learn from each other how God is using such groups within his mission, and how they assist the coming of his Kingdom.

Appendix Two — Conference resolutions on church planting

1992

1 The Conference adopts the report on *Decline and Growth in Methodism* and directs the Home Mission Division to publish a summary version with questions for consideration by local church councils and circuit meetings.

2 The Conference calls upon every circuit in the Connexion seriously and prayerfully to consider ways in which God is calling it to growth; to explore in co-operation with its ecumenical partners the possibility of planting at least one new congregation by the year 2000, and to report on its plans to the District Policy Committee.

3 The Conference encourages every circuit to identify those of its churches where there is evidence of long-term decline, and to report to the District Policy Committee on what action they propose to take.

4 The Conference directs the Home Mission Division, in collaboration with other Divisions, to arrange connexional consultations on church planting as soon as practically possible, and urges each District to ensure that it is appropriately and adequately represented.

5 The Conference directs the Home Mission Division, in consultation with the Property Division and the Ecumenical Committee, to prepare material on different approaches to church planting together with guidelines for circuits wishing to establish new congregations.

1993

The Conference reaffirms the need for circuits to consider opportunities for planting new congregations as a means to growth.

Appendix Three —
10 DAWN principles for responsible church planting

The DAWN (Discipling A Whole Nation) approach is a strategic and collaborative approach to church planting and church growth. The faith-goal for Methodism arrived at by the Methodist group attending the first European DAWN Congress in 1992 was 'to establish an appropriate new congregation in every Methodist circuit by the year 2000'. This was echoed in the 1992 Methodist Conference Resolution. (See Appendix Two).

- **Responsible Pluralism:** A given area may have more than one group ministering in it.

- **Mutual Respect:** A participating body considering the possibility of entering a locality where there are existing churches, will consult with representatives of those churches with an attitude of respect.

- **Proximity and Density:** When a group considers entering a locality, it will evaluate and minimize any possible adverse effects due to proximity to an existing group. A dense population may reasonably allow different groups to be closer together than in sparsely populated areas.

- **Unity with Diversity:** There is an intrinsic unity of the Holy Spirit in the Body of Christ. There is legitimacy for diverse structural and doctrinal distinctives within the churches/denominations/groups that co-operate together.

- **Team Spirit and Fellowship:** Workers from different participating bodies working in a given locality are encouraged to arrange for communication and fellowship, to create a team spirit.

- **Sharing Resources:** Each participating body in an area is encouraged to make its resources available to support evangelistic and church planting efforts.

- **Reaching the Unreached:** Participating bodies are encouraged to give priority to areas or groups where there is no resident gospel witness or church.

- **Reconciliation:** Every effort should be made to resolve conflicts between participating bodies consistent with Matthew 18:15-17 and 1 Corinthians 6:1-8.

- **Church/Parachurch Relationship:** The centrality of local church life is emphasised, and the supportive ministry of parachurch organisations recognised. Consultation between the two groups is encouraged.

- **Common Planning:** Common planning amongst participating bodies should be done periodically, and each group's plans shared.

Bibliography

Core Reading
Church Planting (1. Models for mission in the Church of England) Bob Hopkins (Grove Books)

Church Planting (2. Some experiences and challenges) Bob Hopkins (Grove Books)

Planting Tomorrow's Churches Today Martin Robinson, Stuart Christine (Monarch)

Other Books/Leaflets
A World Apart—Creating a Church for the unchurched Martin Robinson (Monarch/CPAS)

Church Planting for a greater harvest Peter Wagner (Regal Books)

DAWN 2000 Jim Montgomery (Highland)

Planting New Churches Ed. Bob Hopkins (Eagle)

Radical Church Planting Roger Ellis, Roger Mitchell (Crossway)

Planning for Growth—20 questions for growing churches (Study booklet based on 1992 Methodist Conference report on Decline and Growth in Methodism) (Methodist Church Home Mission, 1992)

Circuit Policy-making Guide (Sharing in God's Mission Study Guide Four) (Methodist Church Home Mission, 1994)

Testimony
Ten New Churches Ed. Roger Forster (MARC Europe)

In the Crucible Robert Warren (Highland)

On the Anvil Robert Warren (Highland)

Local Ecumenical Projects
Patterns of sharing and commitment between Methodist and United Reformed Churches (Methodist/URC liaison Committee—6th Edition 1990)

Methodists and LEPs (Methodist Church SCLED/Property Division 1993)

Under One Roof: Guidelines (revised 1993) to the Sharing of Church Buildings Act 1969 (CCBI/CTE/CYTUN—expected 1994)